OTHER BOOKS BY EMMA FLANNERY AND TIM FLANNERY

Explore Your World: Weird, Wild, Amazing!

Explore Your World: Deep Dive into Deep Sea

Explore Your World: Weirdest Creatures in Time

Explore Your World: Creepiest Crawly Critters

EMMA FLANNERY   TIM FLANNERY

It's time to put on your scuba gear and dive into the wonderful world of...

SENSATIONAL SHARKS

Hardie Grant
CHILDREN'S PUBLISHING

Illustrated by
KATIE MELROSE

MEET THE MIGHTY SHARK

Do you spy a shark swimming speedily towards you? As the shark swims, it moves its tail side to side, gliding through the water with its torpedo-shaped body and keeping its mouth, full of sharp teeth, open and ready to welcome a meal. You may feel your body tense, and wonder:

WILL THAT MEAL BE ME?

2

Most humans are tremendously scared to be in the water with a shark. Many sharks are fearsome and have several superpowers that help them find their prey. Luckily, you don't need to worry – you're not a shark's favourite meal!

Sharks are a special kind of fish that have many curious features, such as toothy skin and a skeleton that's not made of bone.

Our oceans and rivers are home to over ONE BILLION sharks, across 500 species of different shapes and sizes. Over 70 per cent of the Earth's surface is covered in water. This means sharks have much more space to live in than you or me.

Sharks are amazing animals. They've been around for a long time – they are the **ancient rulers of the ocean**.

WHERE TO FIND A SHARK

There are more than 500 different kinds of sharks, but they won't all bump into one another! The ocean isn't one big balloon of salty water that's the same in every spot; it is home to many different places for sharks to live in, and some sharks can be very picky about where they live! There may be a shark living near you ...

4

Did you know that ninjas live in the deep dark sea? The **NINJA LANTERN SHARK** is a secretive shark that stayed hidden from humans until its discovery in 2010. Its long, slender body grows to 45 centimetres and it has tiny sharp teeth that are almost see-through. This shark has one very spectacular superpower: it can make light with its pitch-black body! Scientists think this helps the shark blend in with the very small amount of light in the deep ocean, like a cloak of invisibility! With it, the shark can avoid danger, or sneak up on its next meal.

The scientist who named the ninja lantern shark had help from her eight-year-old cousins.

HOW COOL!

BULL SHARKS sometimes bump into humans when they venture into very shallow water or freshwater rivers. They have a stocky body with a rounded nose, and grow to around 2 to 3 metres long. Most sharks need to live in salt water so they can keep enough salt in their bodies, but bull sharks are an exception. They have kidneys that can recycle salt and a specialised gland near their butt that stops salt leaking out.

AMAZING!

TIGER SHARKS are at home in tropical waters and can grow more than 4 metres long, making them the second-largest shark that is a predator, after the great white shark. Young tiger sharks sport faint stripes on their backs. Tiger sharks aren't fussy when it comes to food. They eat fish, other sharks, crabs, turtles and seals – anything they can get their teeth into, including baby birds, metal, plastic and even porcupine spines!

The **PACIFIC SLEEPER SHARK** got its name because it moves sluggishly, like it is falling asleep in the water! These sharks venture into the chilly waters at the very top of the globe in both the Arctic and Pacific oceans. The Pacific sleeper shark can reach over 6 metres long and has small fins for its body size. It swims in a sneaky fashion, and can take its prey by surprise. Pacific sleeper sharks are not picky with their food – they will eat most things that come their way.

FIVE THINGS THAT MAKE A SHARK A SHARK

1

Unlike most fish, you won't find a single bone in a shark's body. Instead, sharks have **skeletons made of cartilage**. Squeeze the tip of your nose – it's got cartilage too! Cartilage is more flexible and softer than bone, but it holds its shape. It is also lighter, so it helps a shark swim super fast.

2

We breathe in air and get oxygen using our lungs, but our lungs won't work underwater. To breathe, sharks have between **five and seven gills** on each side of their head. When a shark swims, water enters its mouth and runs past the gills. Their gills absorb the oxygen that is dissolved in the water.

3

Sharks have **stiff fins** that make them quick and excellent swimmers.

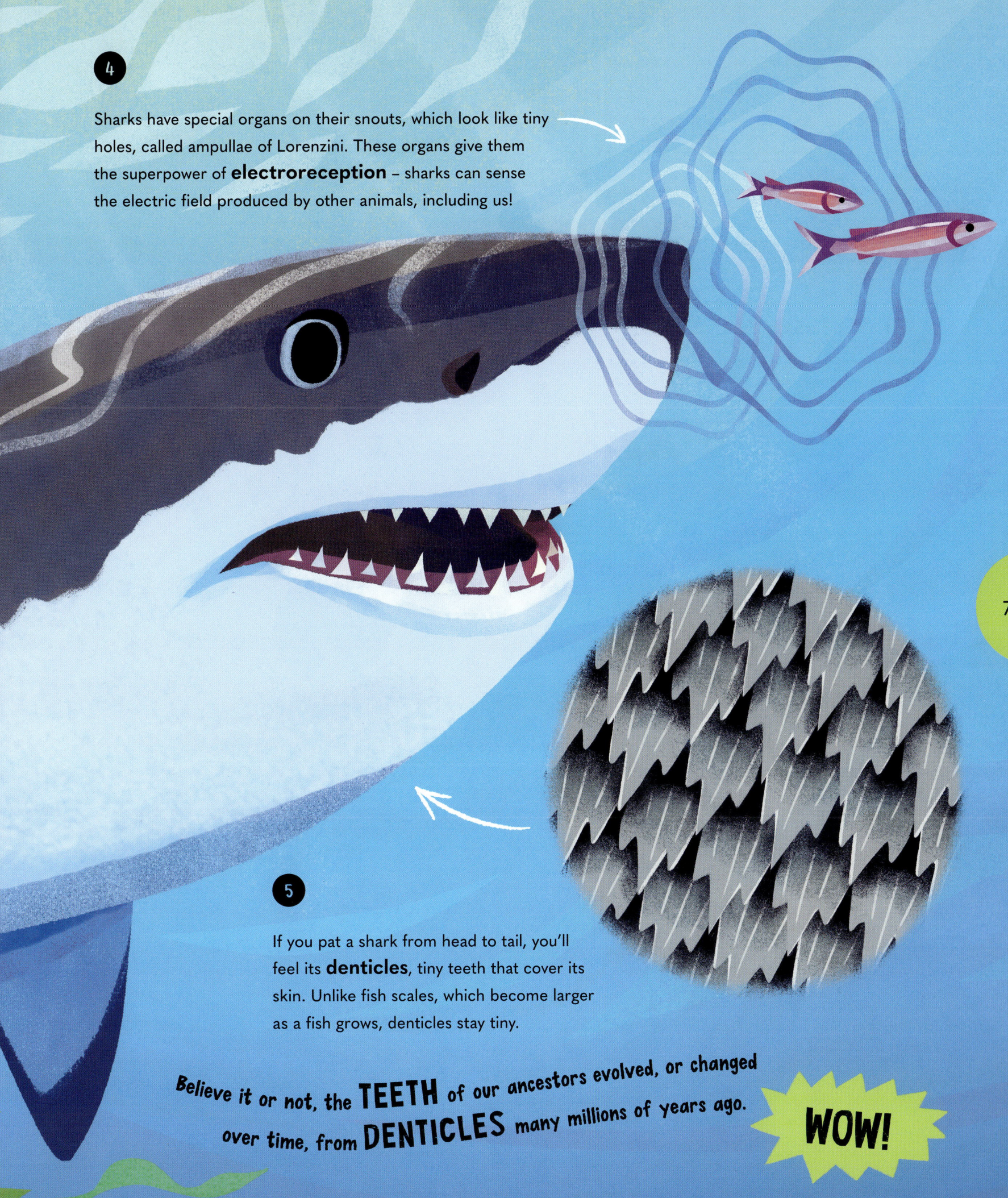

4

Sharks have special organs on their snouts, which look like tiny holes, called ampullae of Lorenzini. These organs give them the superpower of **electroreception** – sharks can sense the electric field produced by other animals, including us!

5

If you pat a shark from head to tail, you'll feel its **denticles**, tiny teeth that cover its skin. Unlike fish scales, which become larger as a fish grows, denticles stay tiny.

Believe it or not, the **TEETH** of our ancestors evolved, or changed over time, from **DENTICLES** many millions of years ago.

WOW!

SHARKS COME IN ALL SHAPES AND SIZES

Different species of sharks can look vastly different to one another. They can be as big as a bus or the size of a banana, depending on where they live.

The whale shark is the size of a SCHOOL BUS!

LET'S MEET SOME OF THE WEIRDEST ONES!

The **DWARF LANTERN SHARK** is the smallest shark in the world. It has large eyes and brown skin with black markings and is a shy critter. It's only been spotted a few times, around the top of South America.

This shark has a special talent, which you might be able to guess from its name: its body lights up like a lantern! Along its belly and fins are little light-producing organs called photophores. During the daytime, the shark's lit-up belly matches the sunshine above and it stays hidden. In dark waters, such as during night-time or in the deep sea, producing light helps attract a yummy critter to eat!

The dwarf lantern shark fits in the palm of an adult human's hand.

Meet the largest fish in the sea, the **WHALE SHARK!** This humungous shark is blue-grey with white spots and likes to live in warmer waters. The whale shark has a mouth with jaws that are 1.5 metres wide – the height of a 12-year-old kid. But don't worry about being swallowed whole by a whale shark; they are filter feeders and so only eat very tiny critters, like plankton and small fish. The whale shark can travel long distances in search of food.

The goblin shark is about the same size as a tiger.

The **GOBLIN SHARK** is named after the mythical goblin creature of Japanese legend. Its skin is a pinkish colour – the only cute thing about it! It has a large shovel-shaped nose and an extendable jaw that is attached to its mouth by flaps of skin. Goblin sharks live in the endless darkness of the deep sea and are the slowpokes of the ocean, but they have the fastest jaws. They drift along, waiting to ambush their prey. When a goblin shark is close enough to a yummy fish, its extendable jaws and needle-like teeth snap forward in an instant.

A SHARK'S SMILE

Shark teeth are **SUPER TOUGH** and are often the only thing left after a shark dies. A tooth can survive for millions of years as a fossil.

In the monstrous mouth of a shark, you will spy oodles of teeth in multiple rows. Unlike grown-up humans, who have just 32 teeth, a shark has hundreds on a never-ending conveyor belt. As soon as a shark loses a tooth from all that chomping, another is ready to replace it. Shark teeth can come in different shapes, depending on what they like to eat.

To chow down on seals and whales, **GREAT WHITE SHARKS** have wide and serrated teeth – handy for sawing into the thick flesh of larger animals.

Filter-feeding sharks, like the **WHALE SHARK, BASKING SHARK** and **MEGAMOUTH SHARK**, have tiny teeth that aren't even used for eating. They suck in huge amounts of sea water, full of tiny critters called plankton, which they sieve through their gills.

SAND TIGER SHARKS have long pointy teeth to catch fast and slippery prey, like bony fish and squid. Their teeth have two prongs jutting out called cusplets.

PORT JACKSON SHARKS have a mouth that looks like a grandma leaning in for a kiss! Their funny-shaped mouths have small teeth at the front and flat teeth at the back that are helpful for grabbing and crushing sea urchins, sea snails, crabs and clams.

FEEDING FRENZY

What all sharks have in common is that they are carnivores and eat other animals. They don't always have to eat fresh meat. Sometimes they scavenge or eat other things. When multiple sharks are excited to eat the same prey, you get a feeding frenzy. They become so excited that they crowd around and make a big splash. Each shark tries to get the biggest bite of the animal before the food is all gone ...

Maybe you've been in a feeding frenzy around a birthday cake!

12

DON'T INVITE
A SHARK
TO DINNER!

Most have no table manners! Sharks can't even chew their food. Instead, most use their sharp teeth to rip off hunks of meat that they then swallow whole.

The **COOKIE CUTTER SHARK** doesn't look very menacing, with its skinny, half-metre-long body, rounded snout and small fins. But when compared with other sharks, it has the biggest teeth for its body size. This shark got its funny name because of how it feeds. It makes its own cookies using its mouth! But instead of chocolate chips, it prefers flesh-flavoured cookies. It suctions its big lips onto the skin of a larger animal, such as a big fish or a dolphin, and then twists around to take a bite – ouch! You know where a cookie cutter shark has been because it leaves a cookie-shaped wound on its prey.

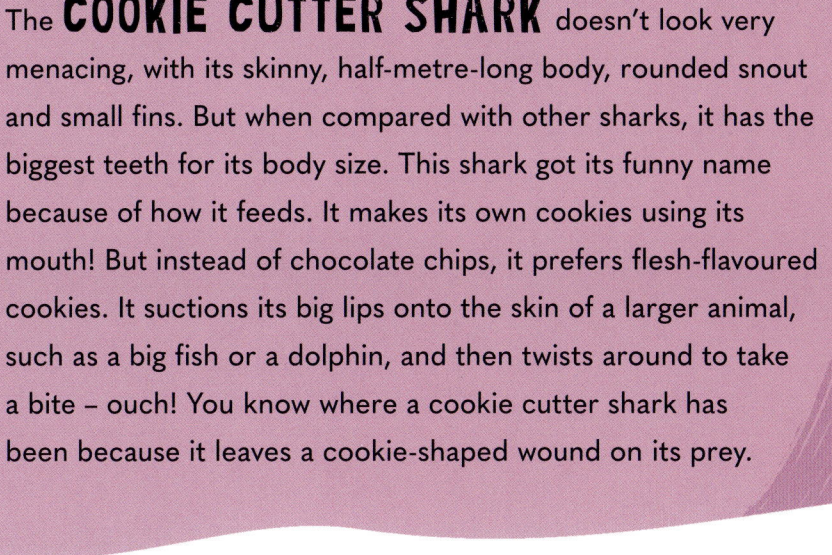

One of the world's largest and creepiest sharks, the **GREENLAND SHARK** is also the slowest moving. Instead of hunting for prey, it scavenges already dead prey, using its super sense of smell to find the stinky rotting bodies of large animals. Ugh! The Greenland shark can grow 7 metres long, and lives in the cold deep sea, blindly bumbling along at 1.2 kilometres per hour, slower than the walking pace of a toddler.

13

The Greenland shark can't see very well because it has wormy parasites that munch on its eyeballs, but it can gulp down a dead seal whole! **PARASITES** are animals that live on or in another animal, causing harm.

Astonishingly, the **BONNETHEAD SHARK** is one of few sharks that like to eat their greens! It is just under a metre in length, lives in the warm shallows off North and South America, and has a head shaped like a shovel. It likes to eat seagrass, but will happily munch on crabs and clams.

MOVE LIKE A SHARK

Sharks move with incredible strength and agility: some can dive as fast as a flash, stop in the blink of an eye and make a tight turn in any direction.

If a shark had no fins, it would go topsy-turvy and roll upside down in the water! Their stiff fins keep them stable, push them forward and help them steer. Sharks also use them to control their depth. There are five types of stiff fins sharks can have:

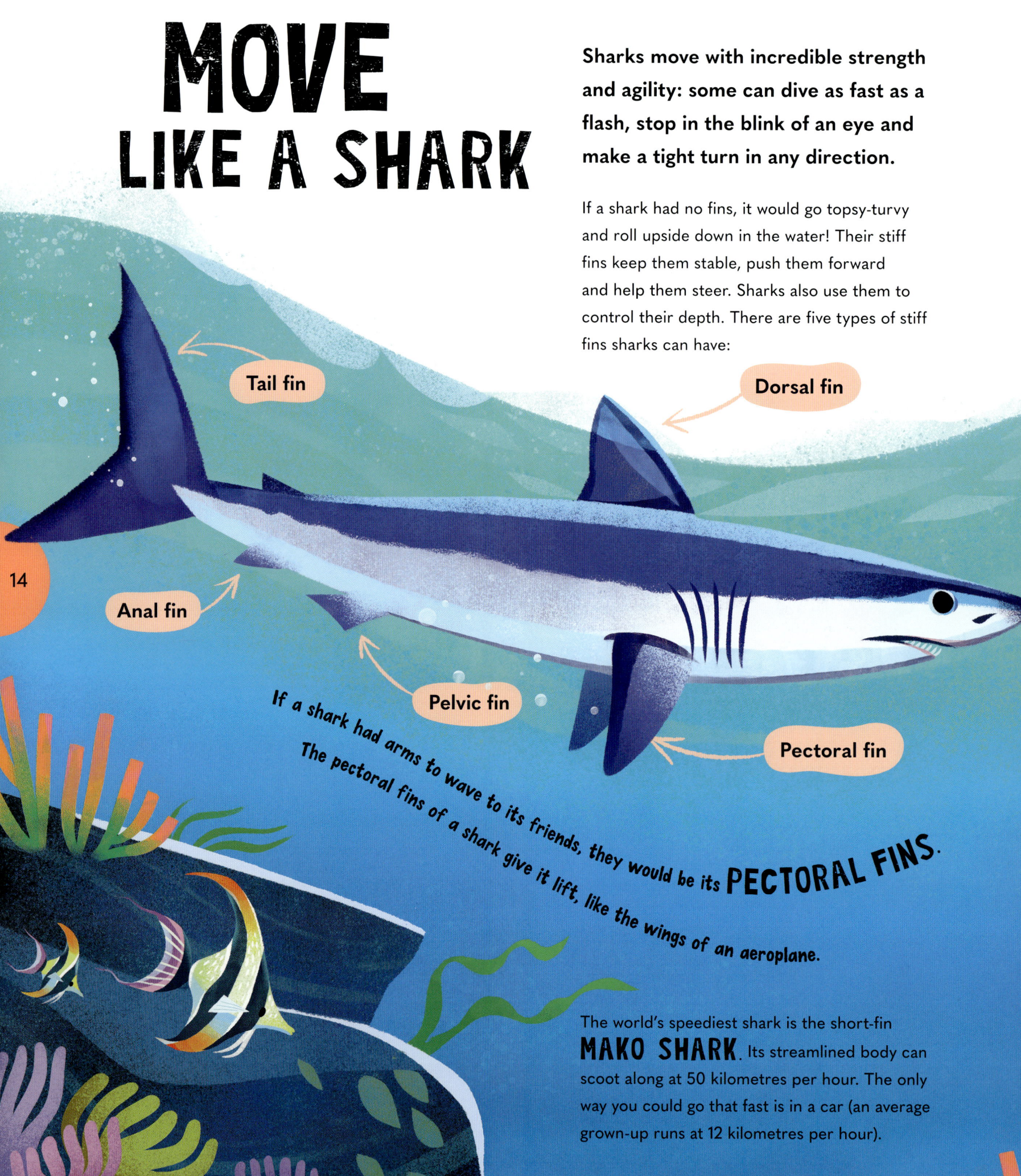

Tail fin

Dorsal fin

Anal fin

Pelvic fin

Pectoral fin

14

If a shark had arms to wave to its friends, they would be its PECTORAL FINS. The pectoral fins of a shark give it lift, like the wings of an aeroplane.

The world's speediest shark is the short-fin **MAKO SHARK**. Its streamlined body can scoot along at 50 kilometres per hour. The only way you could go that fast is in a car (an average grown-up runs at 12 kilometres per hour).

Sharks can migrate or travel huge distances to feed or find a mate. The longest recorded swim is halfway across the surface of the Earth!

Sharks don't just move across the ocean, they also move up and down. Many sharks swim in the depths of the ocean during the day, then migrate to more shallow waters at night.

Sharks have extra oily livers. Because oil is lighter than water, their liver helps them stay buoyant, or afloat. Some sharks even use farts to stay afloat! How stinky! In aquariums, **SAND TIGER SHARKS** have been seen to gulp air at the surface and then let out tiny farts until they are at the right level in the water.

The shark with the longest fin is the **THRESHER SHARK**. Its tail fin can reach 3 metres long and helps the thresher shark swim fast. It is also used to stun prey with a swift slap!

Sharks must keep moving or they will sink to the bottom of the sea.

OH NO!

MASTER HUNTER

Sharks are experts when it comes to finding a meal. Along with their excellent ability to move, sharks have extraordinary senses of sight, sound and smell to hunt. Sharks can see much better than we can in dim light, and can hear and smell better than us underwater. A shark can detect sounds and smells from over 200 metres away. Their sense of smell is especially sensitive – they'll smell the tiniest drop of blood from an injured prey nearby.

Remember, sharks have the superpower of **electroreception** too! It helps them hunt in complete darkness and find prey buried within the sea floor. The special jelly-like tubes in their snout, called ampullae of Lorenzini, detect the electric fields of other animals. Using electroreception, sharks can find completely still or hidden prey – there is no escape.

All animals have an electric field, which comes from the nerves and muscles working in their bodies. Imagine having electroreception – you'd be able to sense your friend's heartbeat when you play hide-and-seek!

Sharks aren't the only animals that use electroreception. Other kinds of fish use it too, including lampreys and lungfishes. The platypus has electroreceptors in its bill to find prey that's hidden in murky water.

If you kick in the water, even a long way from a shark, it will feel the pressure of your kick on its side.

Sharks have a special organ called a **lateral line**, which runs down the sides of their bodies. This helps them pick up changes in water pressure and sense any movement in the water up to 100 metres away.

A MATING MYSTERY

The mating habits of most kinds of sharks remain a mystery because we hardly ever catch them in the act. Most sharks only mate every two to three years and it can be difficult to be at the right spot at the right time to spy on them! A lot of what we do know is from observing captive sharks in an aquarium, as well as from studying the shape of their reproductive organs.

We can look at the underside of a shark's body to tell if it's male or female. Male sharks have **claspers** – two grooved organs that are near the pelvic fins. Female sharks have a **cloaca** – an opening on their belly that leads to their eggs.

To make a baby shark, the female shark's egg and the male shark's sperm must meet. Male sharks will use their claspers to deliver sperm into a female shark's cloaca, so that it reaches her eggs.

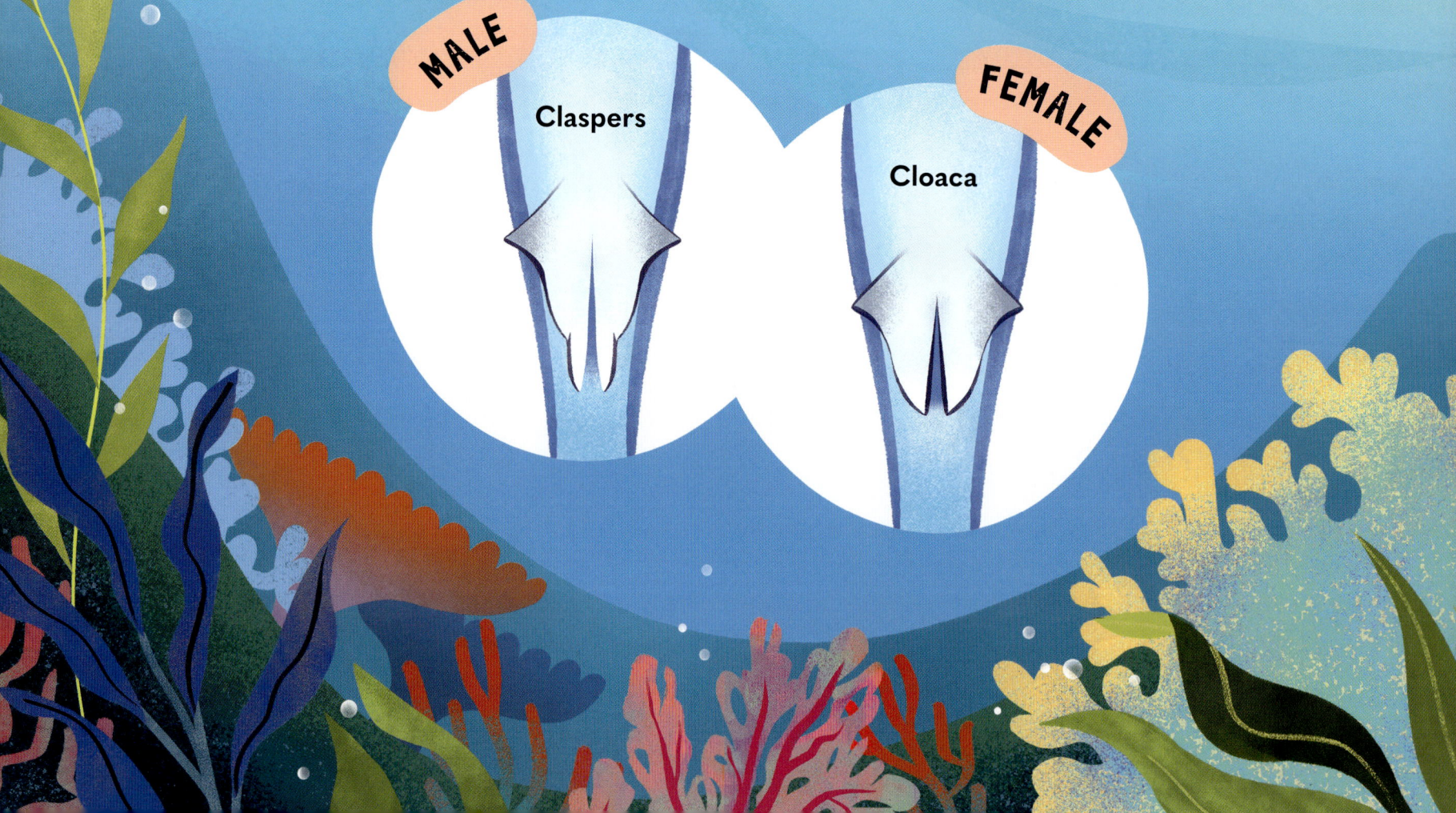

MALE

Claspers

FEMALE

Cloaca

When she's ready to mate, a female shark releases special chemicals in the water called **pheromones**. A male shark will smell these pheromones and know where to find her.

Sometimes a male shark will bite a female shark on the fin when they mate. **OUCH!** But don't worry, many female sharks have much thicker skin than males.

BABY SHARKS

A baby shark is called a pup and different sharks produce pups in different ways.

Sharks like the **PORT JACKSON SHARK** lay eggs, with the baby sharks hatching outside the mother's body.

Other sharks, like the **GREY NURSE SHARK** and the **WHALE SHARK**, have eggs that hatch inside the mother's body.

Next time you are at the beach you might find a washed-up shark egg. Shark eggs come in weird and wonderful shapes, from long spirals to pointed rectangles.

There is even a shark egg called a **MERMAID PURSE** because of its shape!

Some sharks, such as the **BULL SHARK** and the **HAMMERHEAD SHARK**, never hatch from eggs at all – they are born as live young.

Do you think your brother or sister looks **TASTY?**

When still inside their mother, before they are even born, some sharks get very hungry. As soon as a baby shark gets its tiny teeth, it gobbles up other baby sharks in the womb. Usually the largest and strongest baby shark eats the others.

EEK!

The biggest shark pup belongs to the **BASKING SHARK.** As a newborn it can reach a whopping 2 metres long – the height of the tallest basketball player!

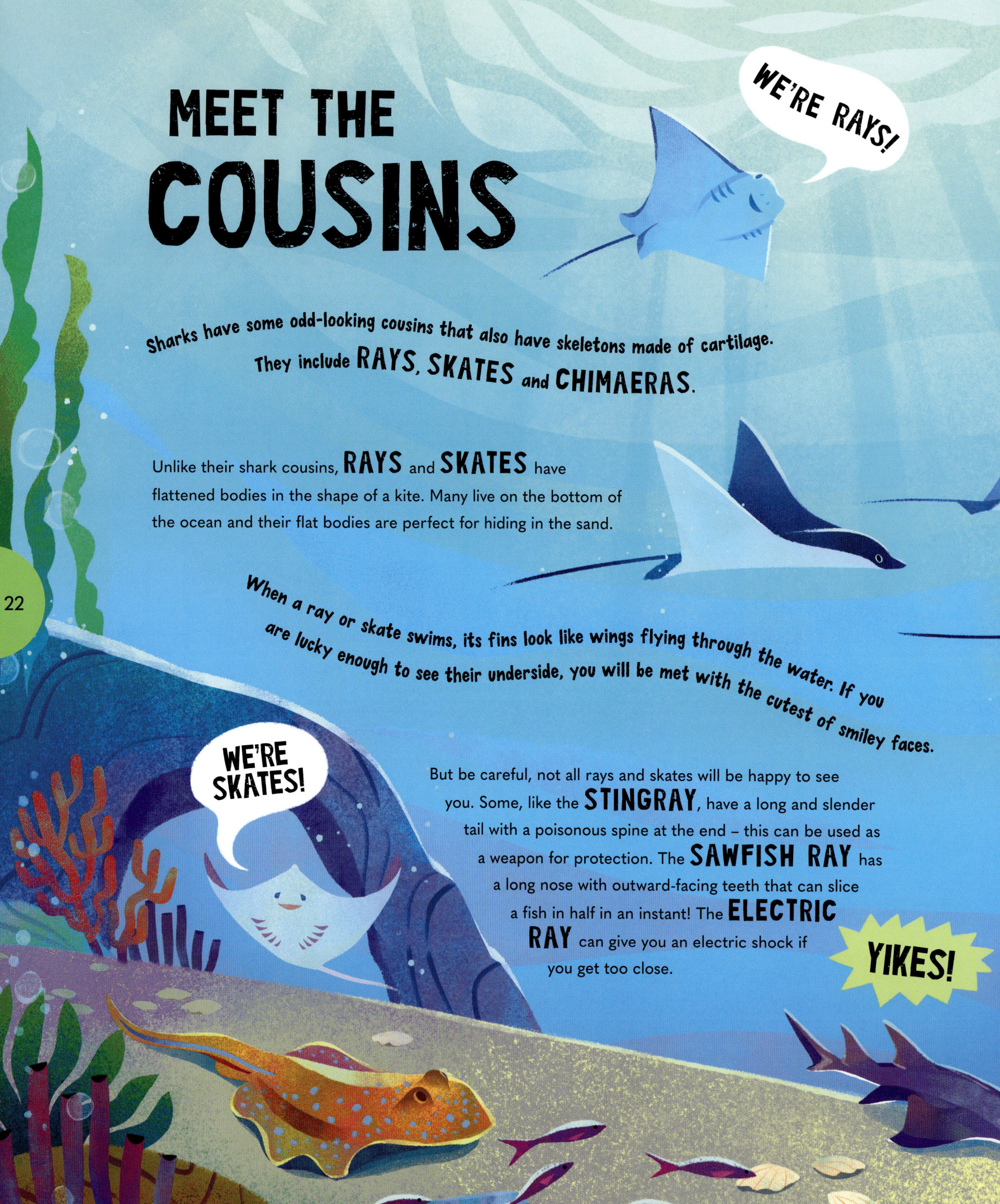

MEET THE COUSINS

WE'RE RAYS!

Sharks have some odd-looking cousins that also have skeletons made of cartilage. They include **RAYS**, **SKATES** and **CHIMAERAS**.

Unlike their shark cousins, **RAYS** and **SKATES** have flattened bodies in the shape of a kite. Many live on the bottom of the ocean and their flat bodies are perfect for hiding in the sand.

When a ray or skate swims, its fins look like wings flying through the water. If you are lucky enough to see their underside, you will be met with the cutest of smiley faces.

WE'RE SKATES!

But be careful, not all rays and skates will be happy to see you. Some, like the **STINGRAY**, have a long and slender tail with a poisonous spine at the end – this can be used as a weapon for protection. The **SAWFISH RAY** has a long nose with outward-facing teeth that can slice a fish in half in an instant! The **ELECTRIC RAY** can give you an electric shock if you get too close.

YIKES!

GIANT MANTA RAYS are gentle ocean giants, and are the largest ray or skate. They have a wingspan of almost 9 metres long and weigh around 1,600 kilograms, as heavy as a small car. The word 'manta' means 'blanket' in Spanish, and this fish sure does look like a big blanket swimming in the water! Luckily, manta rays are way smarter than a wet blanket. In fact, they are one of the smartest cold-blooded fish. Manta rays do incredible acrobatics – somersaults and spirals – when they feed on tiny animals called plankton.

CHIMAERAS look so bizarre that they are also called rat fish, rabbit fish and ghost sharks! Many people have not heard of chimaeras as most live secret lives in deep waters. Chimaeras do not have rough skin or teeth like a shark, instead they have smooth skin and three rows of grinding plates. They also have large eyes and slender tails, and gills that are covered by a single flap. One kind of chimaera, the **ELEPHANT FISH**, even has a funny fleshy snout that it uses to feed on the sandy sea floor!

WE'RE CHIMAERAS!

BIG MEG

Sharks are the ancient rulers of the ocean, and have been on this Earth a very long time. We humans have been around for 200,000 years, but sharks have been around for at least 450 million years! This means sharks were swimming in the oceans long before dinosaurs, and even before there was a single tree on the land.

Long ago, there were many sharks that are no longer alive today. The greatest of them all was **OTODUS MEGALODON**, or **THE MEG** for short.

The biggest of the Meg's 276 teeth was the length of a man's hand and its dorsal fin was as tall as a grown-up.

The Meg was as heavy as 10 elephants.

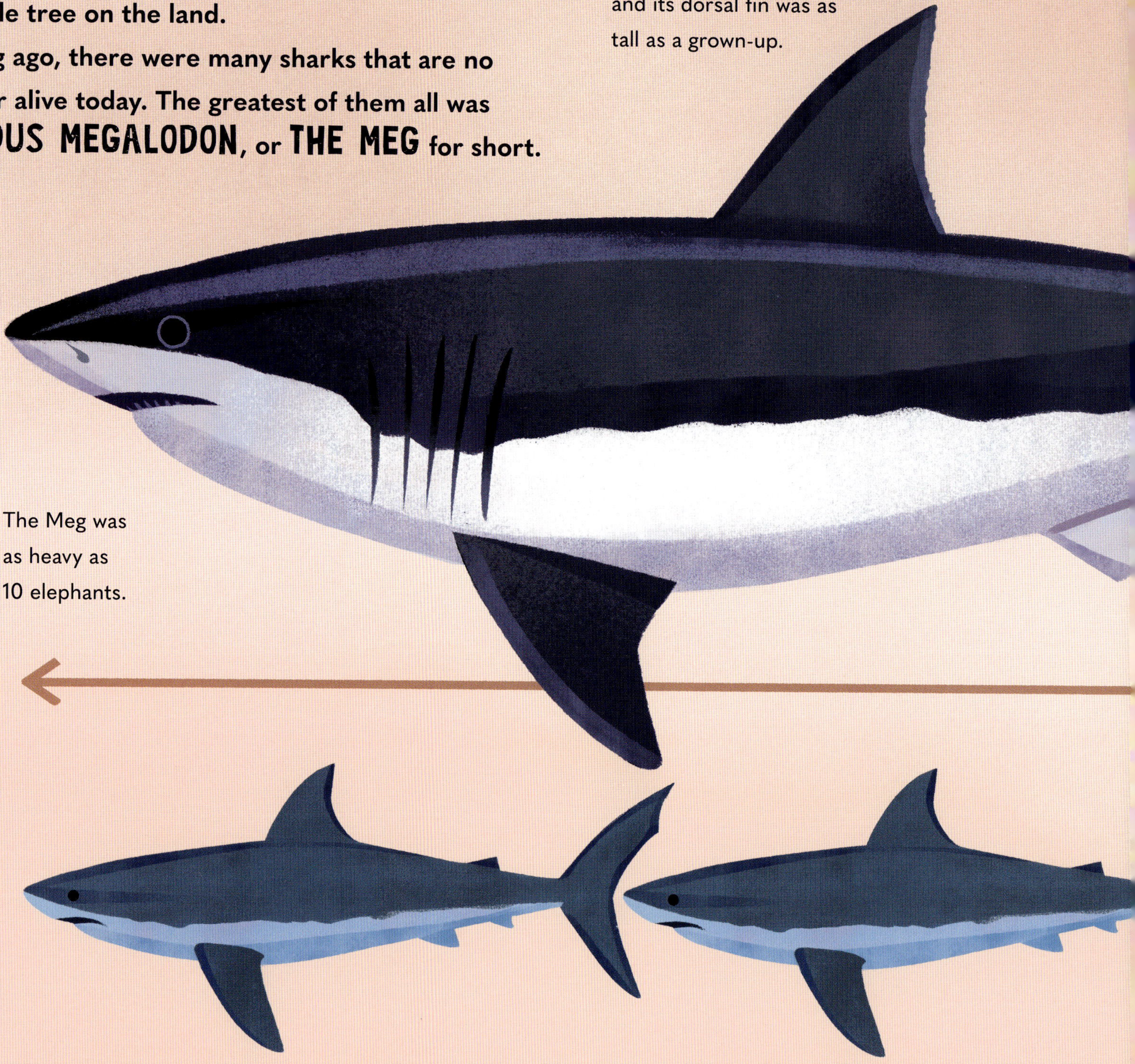

The jaws of the Meg could open almost 3 metres wide, big enough to swallow you and many other friends whole!

Remember the GREENLAND SHARK?

It's the world's oldest vertebrate (an animal with a backbone) and it can live to be 500 years old! These sharks grow very slowly, around a centimetre a year. Unbelievably, they are only grown-ups and ready to have babies when they are around 150 years old!

The Meg had a big appetite and loved to eat whales.

The Meg died out around 4 million years ago and we aren't really sure why. Maybe it was the Earth's cooling climate or maybe they had to compete with the modern great white shark for food. Next time you are at the beach keep your eyes peeled for a giant tooth from the long-gone Meg. Every now and then someone has stumbled across one, including a few five-year-old kids!

The Meg could grow between 15 and 20 metres in length – three times the size of the largest great white shark.

The Meg's bite was three times as powerful as the fearsome *Tyrannosaurus rex*.

INFAMOUS HUMAN-EATING SHARKS

Is there anything more terrifying than being eaten alive? It's no wonder we humans are scared of sharks, but it's important to remember that shark attacks are incredibly rare and often a case of mistaken identity.

News reports and movies can exaggerate shark attacks. The iconic movie *Jaws* was centred on a human-eating shark. Even though *Jaws* was completely made up, it caused so much terror that people were afraid to swim at the beach!

People travel the world as tourists to see sharks in their natural home. If you are brave, you can scuba dive with bull sharks in the tropical waters of Fiji, or cage dive with great white sharks off South Africa.

With its pitch-black eyes, pointy nose and razor-sharp teeth, the **GREAT WHITE SHARK** is one famous fish. It is the villain in many movies, including *Jaws*, but you won't find one at a red-carpet premiere!

The great white shark is the largest fish on Earth that is a predator. An adult great white shark can reach 6 metres long, half the length of a bus. This fearsome shark munches on fish, turtles, seals and even small whales, and is most at home in cooler waters.

Great whites are sneaky sharks: they hide in the depths to surprise prey that is swimming up above. They can swim so fast towards prey on the surface that they jump out of the water, making a huge splash! The great white shark has a reputation for being a man-eater. Even though great white sharks cause the most human deaths of any shark, a falling coconut is more likely to kill you!

PHEW?

OCEANIC WHITE TIPS are also known as sea dogs because they often swim behind ships, hoping for food to be flung overboard. They are around 3 to 4 metres long and are named for the white tips on their paddle-like fins. There's no need to be scared of an oceanic white tip at the beach – they steer clear of shallow water. These sharks live alone but sometimes come together for a feeding frenzy.

If you were on a sinking ship, you'd hope there were no oceanic white tips around. These sharks are famous for eating humans stranded in the middle of the sea. **EEK!**

During wartime in 1945, the USS *Indianapolis* had 1200 men aboard when it was hit by a missile. As the ship sank, survivors were left floating in the Pacific Ocean. Their rescue took four days – and in that time, the ocean white tips had a feeding frenzy, killing many of the survivors.

ARE SHARKS AFRAID OF HUMANS?

Believe it or not, sharks have more reason to be afraid of humans than humans have of sharks. Sharks are responsible for around 10 human deaths a year, and most of the time this is because a shark accidentally mistakes a human for its prey. On the other hand, humans kill around 100 million sharks a year – wowsers! That means every second of every day more than two sharks are killed by humans.

WHY AND HOW DO WE KILL ALL THESE SHARKS?

28

Sometimes sharks die by accident in huge nets that are used for fishing other fish. When an animal dies in a fishing net and is unwanted, it is called **BYCATCH**.

Humans hunt sharks as a sport, and preserve their jaws, teeth and even entire bodies as **trophies**. Scarier-looking sharks, such as the **MAKO SHARK** and **GREAT WHITE SHARK**, are highly prized targets.

29

Humans hunt sharks for food, and many are caught just for their fins. Shark fins are sold for a lot of money and they are used in some parts of the world to make **soup**. Often a shark's fins are removed and its body dumped back in the ocean.

WHAT A WASTE.

WHY ARE SHARKS IMPORTANT?

Even though some sharks look scary, there is a lot we need to thank them for!

Being predators, sharks play an important role in the ocean **food chain** by keeping the numbers of their prey in check. The food chain is all about who eats who in the wild, and sharks are at the top of it. Fewer sharks would mean more of their prey, which can negatively impact the ecosystem of our oceans.

An **ECOSYSTEM** is a finely balanced environment, in which all the living things (plants, animals and other organisms) and non-living things (like rocks and the weather) work together to maintain the system's health.

Climate change affects sharks in many ways. First, a warming ocean impacts their favourite prey, meaning they may have less to eat or must change their diet. As the ocean temperature rises, sharks also could be forced to migrate elsewhere, and they might turn up in unexpected places and eat new types of prey. This can disrupt the food chain. Some sharks like to give birth in shallow waters called nurseries, and climate change can change where these nurseries are. These nurseries can move or be destroyed with a rise in sea levels.

Scientists like sharks too!
Scientists study sharks because sharks don't often get sick and their skin keeps microbes away. By studying sharks, scientists can make medicine and special materials for hospitals. Scientists also copy shark skin to make materials for planes and ships so that they move faster – like a shark!

NOW THAT YOU KNOW MORE ABOUT SHARKS, DON'T FORGET TO SHARE WHAT YOU'VE LEARNED WITH EVERYONE YOU KNOW!

For little Leon

PROFESSOR TIM FLANNERY

is one of the world's leading scientists, explorers and conservationists. He has published more than 30 books, including the award-winning *Here on Earth* and best-selling *Explore Your World* books, many of which he co-wrote with his daughter Emma. He is a frequent presenter on ABC Radio, NPR and the BBC, and has also written and presented several series on the Documentary Channel.

EMMA FLANNERY

is a scientist and writer who has co-written many of the *Explore Your World* books with her father, Tim. Her curiosity for the natural world has seen her travel and work in some of its most wild and interesting places. Her passion for science has an infectious and playful enthusiasm that inspires curiosity in children and adults alike.

KATIE MELROSE

is an illustrator whose love for art and reading was cultivated at a young age by her parents. You'll mostly find her with a brush, but when she's without, she'll be in the kitchen, cooking up a storm and pretending she's a chef – perhaps her second greatest passion in life after illustration.

Hardie Grant acknowledges the Traditional Owners of the Country on which we work, the Wurundjeri People of the Kulin Nation and the Gadigal People of the Eora Nation, and recognises their continuing connection to the land, waters and culture. We pay our respects to their Elders past and present.

Hardie Grant Children's Publishing
Wurundjeri Country
Ground Floor, Building 1, 658 Church Street
Richmond, Victoria 3121, Australia
www.hardiegrantchildrens.com

ISBN: 9781761211706   First published 2023

 A catalogue record for this book is available from the National Library of Australia

Publisher Marisa Pintado
Art Director Pooja Desai
Design Kristy Lund-White
Editorial Joanna Wong with Emma Schwarcz
Production Amanda Shaw
Illustrator Katie Melrose

Printed in China by Leo Paper Group

 MIX
Paper from responsible sources
FSC® C020056

The paper this book is printed on is from FSC®-certified forests and other sources. FSC® promotes environmentally responsible, socially beneficial and economically viable management of the world's forests.

2 4 5 3 1